Secrets
of the Cave

BY DEBORAH LOCK

Series Editor Deborah Lock
Project Editor Camilla Gersh
Editor Pomona Zaheer
Assistant Editor Katy Lennon
Project Art Editor Hoa Luc
Art Editor Rashika Kachroo
US Senior Editor Shannon Beatty
Producer, Pre-production Francesca Wardell
Illustrator Hoa Luc
DTP Designers Anita Yadav, Vijay Kandwal
Picture Researcher Aditya Katyal
Managing Editor Soma B. Chowdhury
Managing Art Editor Ahlawat Gunjan

Reading Consultant
Linda B. Gambrell, Ph.D.

First American Edition, 2015
Published in the United States by DK Publishing
345 Hudson Street, New York, New York 10014

Published in Great Britain by Dorling Kindersley Limited.

A catalog record for this book is available from the Library of Congress.

ISBN: 978-1-4654-2939-1 (Paperback)
ISBN: 978-1-4654-2938-4 (Hardcover)
Printed and bound in China

DK books are available at special discounts when purchased in bulk for sales promotions, premiums, fund-raising,
or educational use. For details, contact: DK Publishing Special Markets, 345 Hudson Street, New York,
New York 10014 or SpecialSales@dk.com

The publisher would like to thank the following for their kind permission to reproduce their photographs:
(Key: a-above; b-below/bottom; c-center; f-far; l-left; r-right; t-top)

1 **Alamy Images**: Glasshouse Images. 5 **Corbis**: Bettmann. 8 **Alamy Images**: Heritage Image Partnership Ltd. (bc); **Dorling Kindersley**: The Natural
History Museum, London (cra); **The Pitt Rivers Museum**, University of Oxford (cr). 9 **Alamy Images**: John Angerson (crb); The Art Gallery Collection (cra).
Dorling Kindersley: The Natural History Museum, London (tr). 12–13 **Getty Images**: Alinari via Getty Images. 15 **Getty Images**: Time & Life Pictures/
Ralph Morse. 16–17 **Getty Images**: DEA/G. Dagli Orti/De Agostini. 19 **Alamy Images**: Hemis (cb); Wild Places/Chris Howes (t). 20 **Dorling Kindersley**: James
Jordan (bl, r). 21 **Dorling Kindersley**: James Jordan (l, r). 23 **Dorling Kindersley**: Geoff Brightling/ESPL-modelmaker. 25 **Corbis**: Hemis/Jean-Daniel Sudres.
27 **Getty Images**: AFP/Lionel Bonaventure. 28–29 **Getty Images**: AFP/Philippe Wojazer. 30 **Corbis**: The Gallery Collection. 34 **Dorling Kindersley**: Simon
Jackson Carter (cl). 35 **Alamy Images**: The Print Collector (cl). 37 **Corbis**. **Dorling Kindersley**: The Royal British Columbia Museum, Victoria, Canada (cl). 37 **Corbis**.
43 **Getty Images**: Gamma-Rapho Via Getty Images/Pierre Briolle. 44–45 **Alamy Images**: Ray Roberts. 46 **Dorling Kindersley**: The Natural History Museum,
London (clb); **Photo Scala, Florence**: DeAgostini Picture Library/Scala, Florence (br). 47 **Dorling Kindersley**: The Natural History Museum, London (tl); The Pitt
Rivers Museum, University of Oxford (cl); The Museum of London (tr). 48 **Science Photo Library**: University Of Manchester/Michael Donne (cla, br). 49 **Science
Photo Library**: University Of Manchester/Michael Donne. 50 **Dreamstime.com**: Robin Kizzar (cr). 51 **Dorling Kindersley**: The Science Museum, London (cra);
Dreamstime.com: William Berry (cr). **Fotolia**: Jose Manuel Gelpi (bc); Mari art (bl). 53 PENGUIN and the Penguin logo are trademarks of Penguin Books Ltd.: Stig
Of The Dump by Clive King © Puffin. 68 **Dorling Kindersley**: The Museum of London (ca, cra).74–75 **Getty Images**: AFP/Lionel Bonaventure. 76–77 **Corbis**:
Reuters/Philippe Wojazer. 79 **Getty Images**: AFP/Lionel Bonaventure. 80–81 **Getty Images**: Gamma-Rapho Via Getty Images/Serge De Sazo. 85 **Alamy Images**:
Robert Harding Picture Library Ltd. 86 **Corbis**: JAI/Amar Grover (cl). 86–87 **Dreamstime.com**: Sommersby (antique photo frame reproduced four times).
87 **Corbis**: Frederic Soltan (cr); Robert Harding World Imagery/Gavin Hellier (tl). **Getty Images**: Seth Joel (bl). 88 **Dorling Kindersley**: The Natural History
Museum, London (cla). 92–93 **Getty Images**: Alinari via Getty Images. 94–95 **Getty Images**: The LIFE Picture Collection/Ralph Morse. 97 **Corbis**: Reuters/
Philippe Wojazer. 99 **Getty Images**: AFP/Pierre Andrieu. 101 **Getty Images**: AFP. 103 **Corbis**: The Gallery Collection. 105 **Getty Images**: Gamma-Rapho Via
Getty Images/Serge De Sazo. 106 **Dreamstime.com**: Somartin (cb). 106–107 **Dreamstime.com**: Dmitrii Kiselev (b). 108 **Dreamstime.com**: Aleksandr Evseev (tl).
113 **Getty Images**: DEA/A. Dagli Orti/De Agostini. 117 **Alamy Images**: Glasshouse Images. 120 **Getty Images**: Time & Life Pictures/Ralph Morse.
121 **Getty Images**: Gamma-Rapho via Getty Images/Jerome Chatin.

Jacket images: Front: **Corbis**: Reuters/Philippe Wojazer; **Dorling Kindersley**: The Museum of London (clb/spear).
Photo Scala, Florence: DeAgostini Picture Library/Scala, Florence (clb/burin); Back: **Getty Images**: Alinari Archives (t);
Spine: **Getty Images**: AFP/Jeff Pachoud (b).**Endpapers: Dorling Kindersley**: The Royal British Columbia Museum, Victoria, Canada

All other images © Dorling Kindersley
For further information see: www.dkimages.com

A WORLD OF IDEAS:
SEE ALL THERE IS TO KNOW
www.dk.com

Contents

DISCLAIMER

This narrative has been inspired by the cave paintings of Lascaux and other caves in the south of France during the Upper **Paleolithic** Age.

Because of the lack of written evidence, **archeologists**, scientists, and other researchers can only guess how **prehistoric** people might have lived.
The discoveries of human and animal skeletons and **artifacts** (objects made by humans) at prehistoric sites as well as the markings on cave walls provide clues, but not all the answers.

There are a variety of theories about the way people lived in prehistoric times. The facts may have been different.

The photographs of the paintings used throughout this book are mostly taken from inside Lascaux cave (or show the reconstructed images at Lascaux II).
The "handprint" and the "Sorcerer" are from other prehistoric caves in southern France.

What you read in this book might be true!

Don't believe everything you read!

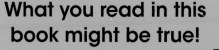

LOCATION

After humans evolved in Africa six million years ago, they spread across Europe as far as Britain, Germany, and Russia, and into Asia. In southern Europe, groups of people began to make and use a range of tools. Prehistoric sites and decorated caves reveal some of their secrets about how they lived.

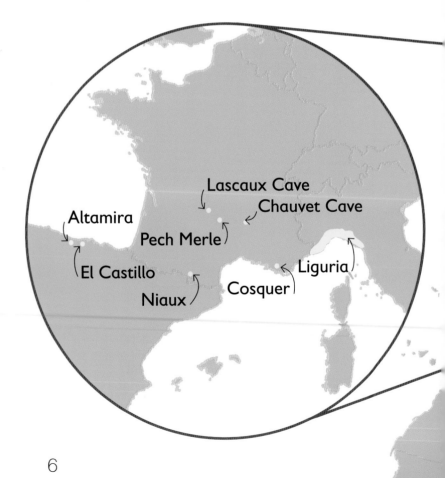

Lascaux Cave

Chauvet Cave

Altamira

Pech Merle

El Castillo

Liguria

Niaux

Cosquer

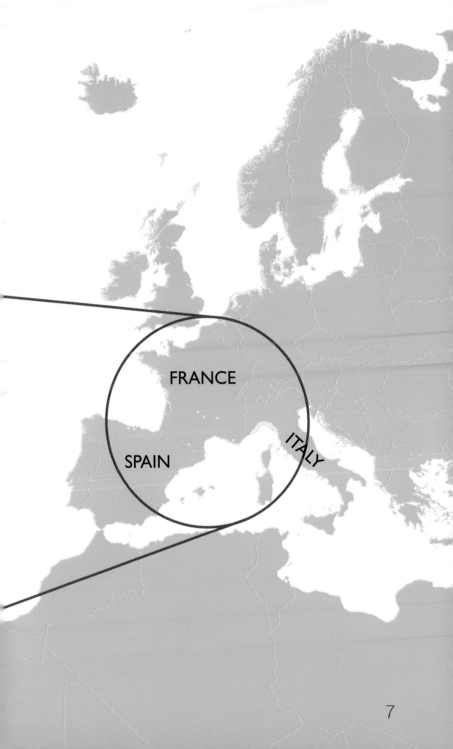

FRANCE

SPAIN

ITALY

Prehistoric Time Chart

PALEOLITHIC 2.6 MYA (MILLION YEARS AGO)–10,000 YEARS AGO

LOWER PALEOLITHIC 2.6 MYA–300,000 years ago

2.6 million years ago
Homo habilis, the first of the *Homo* genus, appears; he chips flakes off pebbles to form rough tools for chopping, scraping, or cutting.

MIDDLE PALEOLITHIC 300,000–30,000 years ago

200,000 years ago
Homo sapiens, the first modern human, appears; he uses the "prepared-core technique" for the first time. In this method, a core is carefully chipped on one side to produce a flake of a certain size and shaped with one blow.

UPPER PALEOLITHIC 50,000–10,000 years ago

33,000–29,000 years ago
Aurignacian period: people begin to use a wide variety of flint and bone tools, including the burin (see pp46–47) for carving, to make the earliest known cave art and figurative art.

27,000–19,000 years ago
Gravettian period:
people hunt large animals in groups
and create bone and shell jewelry
and figurines called "Venuses."

21,000–18,000 years ago
Solutrean period:
people create finely carved blades
and arrowheads in the shape of
laurel leaves and use bone needles
to sew clothes.

17,000–11,500 years ago
Magdalenian period:
people use elaborate tools made of carved
bone and antler and reach a high standard
of cave painting in sites such as Lascaux.

10,000–7,000 years ago
People begin to use tiny carved
tools called microliths.

c.7,000 years ago
People begin farming and
are able to create permanent
settlements. They use small
cutting tools such as adzes.

PALEOLITHIC
UPPER PALEOLITHIC
50,000–10,000 years ago

MESOLITHIC
10,000–7,000
YEARS AGO

NEOLITHIC
7,000–5,000
YEARS AGO

CHAPTER ONE
Discovery

In southwest France in September 1940, four teenage boys were looking for their dog, which had disappeared from view. As they searched, the boys stumbled upon an opening to a cave. This moment marked the discovery of one of the sites for some of the oldest paintings in the world. Lascaux in the wooded hills above the Vézère River became a famous prehistoric landmark! The boys returned to explore the caves in secret. Six days later, they then decided to tell their schoolteacher.

The French archeologist Henri Breuil was the first to study this site at Lascaux. He copied the paintings and tried to explain the meanings behind them. Like all archeologists, he tried to understand the stories of what happened in the cave and piece together the experiences of the early people who had drawn and first seen the paintings. How long ago had they lived? Why had they painted these pictures? What did they do in their daily lives?

Archeologists can never know exactly what happened because the past is lost but by collecting evidence, they can re-create and reconstruct what might have happened. Their work is like tackling a large jigsaw puzzle with pieces missing that they continue to search for. Every now and then, they discover some vital pieces to add to the picture further.

11

The Lascaux cave network is an impressive discovery. For more than 700 feet, steep passageways branch off and open up into chambers of various sizes. The main cavern is a large 66-foot-wide open space with the ceiling towering 16 feet above. Over tens of thousands of years, rainwater dripping through cracks dissolved the soft limestone rock, creating these spaces.

However, it wasn't the network itself that fascinated the archeologists but the high-quality artistic markings and images on the rough, uneven walls. Shining their flashlights over the walls revealed larger-than-life prehistoric animals in colored paintings, strange symbols and patterns, and scratch-mark **engravings**. More than 600 painted and drawn animals and symbols along with 1,500 engravings have been counted. Researchers concluded that this cave had been a gathering place for the early people to witness the performance of hunting and magical **rituals**.

13

When first discovered, many objects were found abandoned on the cave floor. These included the artists' tools and everyday objects, such as lamps, reindeer antlers, flake blades, and scattered bones. These added to the excitement of the discovery for here were items that could expand our knowledge about how our prehistoric ancestors lived and developed.

These objects also helped the archeologists suggest a date for when the Lascaux cave had been actively used: the later stages of the Stone Age, also known as the Upper Paleolithic Age. This is a period that is thought to have lasted tens of thousands of years, but these paintings have been dated toward the end. A fragment from a spearhead in one of the chambers was dated around 17,000BCE (Before Common Era). The style of most of the paintings though seemed to match those from other caves nearby from around 15,000BCE. These artworks had been painted over the top of other older paintings and engravings. The researchers suggest the Lascaux cave was most actively used during these 2,000 years.

The people who lived during this time have been called the Magdalenians. They were successful groups of hunter-gatherers, with a culture known for its developments in toolmaking and artistic techniques.

During the 1950s, the Lascaux cave became a very popular tourist attraction. Artificial lighting lit up the paintings, and 100,000 visitors traipsed through the site each year, gazing at and admiring the artwork. However, the colors on the paintings began to fade under the hot lights, and the carbon dioxide from people's breath caused layers of lichens and crystals to grow over the walls. The quality of the paintings was being ruined. Something had to be done or else the magnificent paintings, symbols, and engravings would vanish. In 1963, the caves were once again closed up.

Why did the
Lascaux cave
have to be closed
to tourists?

Only a handful of people, mostly
scientists, are now allowed to enter,
and only for a few days each year.
Their time inside the cave is precious,
and eerily silent in the glow of their
flashlights through the darkness.
One of their projects was to restore
the original entrance, which they
completed in 1999. For the first time
in 15,000 years, sunlight once again
entered the cave.

VISIT THE WORLD-FAMOUS LASCAUX CAVES

The Grotte de Lascaux World Heritage Site in France is actually several caves containing marvelously preserved paintings that were made by people 17,000 years ago. They show bison, stags, horses, and bulls. They are among the finest examples of prehistoric art in existence.

Painted Gallery

Great Hall of the Bulls

Main Gallery

N

S

LASCAUX II

Although the Lascaux cave is not open to the public because the paintings are too delicate, exact replicas of two of the caves, the Great Hall of the Bulls and the Painted Gallery, can be seen nearby at Lascaux II.

LE THOT

A visit to this prehistoric "theme park" will complement your trip to the cave, with dioramas of prehistoric scenes, live animals like those depicted in the paintings, and a movie explaining how Lascaux II was made. It's fun for the whole family!

NATIONAL MUSEUM OF PREHISTORY

A small detour will bring you to this museum in the tiny, picturesque village of Les Eyzies-de-Tayac. It contains all the most important artifacts found in the Lascaux caves and elsewhere in France. It is not to be missed!

Unusual Suspects

About two million years ago in Africa, the *Homo* genus evolved from apelike ancestors. If any of these early suspects lined up here look familiar, it is because we are closely related to them all.

Homo erectus
1.8 MYA–300,000 years ago
H. erectus had a large face, powerful build, and upright stance (from which he got his name).

Homo habilis
1.9–1.6 MYA (million years ago)
H. habilis had a big brain and was smart enough to make tools.

Homo heidelbergensis
800,000–200,000 years ago
H. heidelbergensis had a
very large brain and was
known to hunt elephants
and rhinos.

Homo neanderthalensis
200,000–30,000 years ago
A cave dweller and expert
hunter, H. neanderthalensis
was thought to have lived
alongside Homo sapiens.

Introducing... *Homo sapiens*

Early *Homo sapiens* possessed several important physical features that gave them unique abilities, such as walking upright and sophisticated thinking. These provided a distinct evolutionary advantage over other species.

large skull to accommodate big brain

short, narrow pelvis supports upper body and enables the body to tilt, maintaining balance when walking

flexible hands and thumbs allow precision grip

well-developed arches and wide heels allow the foot to push off with toes and absorb the forces of walking

large big toes aligned with other toes allow the foot to push off

barrel-shaped ribcage to allow torso to bend and the arms to swing freely to aid balance

curve of the spine helps with balance and allows the spine to bend when walking

short arms, since they are not needed for walking

large knees support increased weight on legs

long thigh bone also helps with balance

CHAPTER TWO
Wild Animals

By 17,000BCE, the ice sheets began to melt across northern Europe. The vast glaciers of the last ice age were thawing. Rivers filled with meltwater and carved their way through the landscape. In the prehistoric forests and valleys of France, the climate was still cool but seasonal. Evergreen conifer trees provided homes for birds. Moss and grasses covered the valleys, as they do in the arctic tundra today. This provided food for the herds of grazing animals passing through on their **migrations**.

Reindeer were frequent visitors during winter and spring on their short yearly migration north for the summer to avoid the biting insects. Their thick outer coats created air spaces that insulated them from the cold and kept them afloat as they swam across icy cold rivers.

Red deer and elk roamed in the forests. Their woolly underlayer of fur kept them warm. Saika antelope also had large air sacs in their noses that warmed up the cold air as they breathed in.

Horses also followed a migratory trail. Rather like Prezewalski's wild horses found in Mongolia today, these prehistoric horses had small heads, short legs with narrow hooves, and round bellies. Most had a brown coat with a black mane and tail, but some were darker—almost black—and others had leopardlike spots. The herds began arriving in the valleys from early spring. They grazed throughout the summer, and then moved south again at the beginning of fall.

Among these horses were also aurochs (wild cattle). These were larger than cattle today, towering over a human at six and a half feet at the shoulder. They could quickly become aggressive, had huge strength, and stampeded with remarkable speed. Their sweeping horns added to their bold and mighty appearance.

Another huge visitor to the grassy river valleys were the steppe bison. With a mass of thick black hair on their shoulder humps, these seemed even taller than the aurochs. Their short forelegs and powerful long hindlegs supported their bulky bodies as they chewed on the grasses, charged at each other, or ran from danger. Protruding from their heads were long horns with curved-back tips, which were up to three feet apart. These came in useful to prove their strength when bulls fought over a mate during the rutting season.

28

As the glaciers melted and forests replaced the mossy plains, the bison abandoned the area and moved northeast to find their food.

What happens during the rutting season?

Cave bears, cave hyenas, and wild cats, such as cave lions and leopards, had once roamed the area when the ice sheets covered northern Europe. They found shelter in the caves, leaving scratch marks on the walls and chewed bones. They moved away as the numbers of wolves and humans increased because they were all competing for the same food. The wolves were smaller and did not require as much food as these larger carnivores. The wolves' pack-hunting tactics also made them more successful.

Other woolly fur beasts stayed

30

around a little longer. During the time of the early Magdalenian people, there were sightings of muskox and woolly rhinoceros. Completely covered in thick, shaggy coats, they were ideally adapted to the cold. The undercoat of the muskox kept out both the cold and water. The rough hair draped down almost to the ground to keep out the snow and the rain. Their hooves stopped them from sinking into the snow. During the rutting season, the bulls (males) let out a strong smell. Like bison, they lived in large herds.

Both beasts grazed on the grass, lichens, and mosses. The rhinos had a broad front lip to tear up the shrubby shoots. They swung their long flattened horns from side to side to push away the snow to uncover them. Just as rhinos do today, they lived either alone or in very small family groups.

The largest of all the woolly animals were the mammoths. Weighing over 10 tons, mammoths towered 16 feet high over the other animals. Not only did their thick fur protect them from the cold, but also they had four inches of solid fat under their skin that kept in the warmth. Their extra-long tusks curled upward to a length of 15 feet for a male.

Like African elephants today, woolly mammoths came together to migrate

as a herd during the spring and scattered during the summer, grazing in the grassy valleys. Then they came together for the migration back in the fall. During the winter, they sheltered in a herd together in the forest, browsing on twigs, bark, leaves, and branches on the trees. Their massive cheek teeth were excellent for grinding the tough, dry food.

Most of these large animals are now extinct. As the ice melted, the climate warmed, the forests grew, the mossy tundra and grasslands disappeared, and these animals had to find other feeding grounds better suited to them in the north and east. Some of them, such as the mammoths and rhinos, could not survive in the fast-changing environment. Never again would such an abundance of large animals and migrating herds live in Europe.

33

Field Guide to the Animals of Lascaux

Paleolithic wall paintings are filled with animals. Many of these animals are similar to modern animals, although most of the actual species are extinct. Here are a few of the animals depicted.

Auroch

This was the ancestor of today's cattle, although it was a bit larger. It was eventually hunted into extinction. The last auroch was killed in 1627.

DATE Pleistocene (2.6 million to 11,700 years ago)
SIZE 10 ft (3 m) long
LOCATION Europe, Asia, North Africa

Horse

Horses have changed very little since prehistoric times. From about 10,000 to 500 years ago, they were extinct in North America but have existed continuously in the region of Lascaux for millions of years.

DATE Pliocene (5.3 to 2.6 million years ago) to present
SIZE 8¼ ft (2.5 m) tall
LOCATION Worldwide

Megaloceros

The *Megaloceros* was one of the largest deer ever known. It was about the size of a modern-day moose. Its antlers were used by the people of Lascaux to craft tools.

DATE Late Pliocene to late Pleistocene
SIZE 8¾ ft (2.7 m) long
LOCATION Europe, Asia

Woolly Mammoth

Mammoths were much like modern elephants in appearance—their DNA is almost identical to that of modern elephants—but their tusks were much longer and curved inward.

DATE Pliocene to late Pleistocene
SIZE 16½ ft (5 m) tall
LOCATION North America, Europe, Asia, Africa

Woolly Rhinoceros

The woolly rhinoceros was about the size of a large white rhino today. It had a thick coat of long, shaggy hair, and a pair of horns that curved backward.

DATE Pleistocene
SIZE 12¼ ft (3.7 m) long
LOCATION Europe, Asia

CHAPTER THREE
Hunters

The Magdalenians are known as the reindeer hunters because the plentiful supply of reindeer were their main source of food. However, they had plenty of other grazing herd animals such as horses, deer, aurochs, and bison to hunt as well. These animals, though, were huge, aggressive, and tough to kill. The people had to develop their hunting tools and tactics to succeed.

Because the animals passing through their areas were on seasonal migrations, the hunters changed their tactics each season to suit. During spring and fall, when most of the animals were migrating, hunters from a number of clans would join together. These large groups guaranteed a high number of kills. The shallower fords in the river were ideal places where the hunters could **ambush** the reindeer as they crossed.

They hunted in small groups in the summer and winter, as the clans spread out across the area.

The Magdalenians are known for their development of a range of tools made from stone, bone, and reindeer antlers. These tools were designed to be light to carry. They developed tools that were used for specific tasks. For hunting, they crafted small triangular-shaped blade flakes and leaf-shaped bone points set into bone, antlers, or wood to make spears.

Blade flakes were thin pieces of rock with a triangular or trapezoid side-on shape. To get the precise shape, a hammer made from antler was slammed down into an upright flint, which was positioned above the rock. The force of the hammer's blow punched the upright flint into the rock, creating a shock wave. A long, delicate blade flake broke away. These blades were thinner, longer, and sharper than those made just by directly hitting the rock with a hammer.

These blade flakes were then shaped into a range of different tools such as knives, scrapers for removing animal hides, spear tips, and borers for drilling holes.

Other stone tools included burins for carving bone, antler, or wood into tools and chiseling out holes or making hooks. The sharp, angled point could also be used to make interesting designs on tool handles. Some tools were designed to be multipurpose—a scraper at one end and a burin on the other. Tools like these were held like a pencil.

What technique was used to make long blade flakes?

Sharper still were bone or antler points. Their tips were shaped to have deadly sharpness. These were used for hunting animals, catching fish, shooting birds, and as spikes for animal traps. Antler points were thinned at the base to slot securely into wooden handles (shafts) to make strong and powerful spears. These would have been fixed with cord and glued with sticky sap from trees. To add power and precision, a separate wooden spear thrower called an atlatl was used. A hole at the back of the spear was inserted into the hook on the spear thrower. When thrown, the spear could go even farther in a more accurate direction.

Harpoons were also carved out of bone with barbed points that stuck out. These points gave a harpoon many hooklike edges on the same tool.

These hooks tore into an animal's flesh as the harpoon was thrust into its side. This prevented the harpoon from falling out, which would have caused the animal to lose blood. Notches at the base were for attaching a cord to a wooden shaft. The use of the shaft gave the harpoon more force when it entered the animal. The harpoon would break off but stay connected by the cord to the shaft, slowing down the escaping injured animal and allowing the hunter to catch up with the animal.

Magdalenian hunters used a variety of hunting strategies. The hunters used the natural environment of rivers, valleys, and cliffs to their advantage. They would ambush the migrating herds at weak points on their migration, such as river crossings or in narrow places. They would also startle a herd and drive them off the top of rock cliffs into valley pits below.

Causing a **stampede** to create confusion among the horses or aurochs was another tactic. Like a pack of hungry wolves, some of the hunters would startle the herd with screams and yells. As the panicked herd stampeded, the hunters would then separate a small group of six to twelve animals. These would be intercepted farther up the valley by another group of hunters. This second band would drive the animals up against the base of a rock cliff, or chase them into a corral-like enclosure. The trapped animals would then be killed. Archeologists studying hunting sites have found mostly adult animal remains. This shows that the hunters were selective, killing only adult animals and releasing the younger ones to rejoin the herd. The hunters knew that these younger ones would grow up to have babies of their own, so that there would always be a plentiful and continual supply of food.

When food was plentiful during the migration seasons, the hunters only took what they needed from the animal carcasses. During the winter, however, more meat was taken off the animals and stored.

For a group of twenty-five people, one reindeer would provide a meal for one day. A horse provided meat for five days, and an auroch for seven days. If the hunters caught a male

bison, it could feed the group for ten days, while a single mammoth kill could keep the group going for well over a month.

The Magdalenian hunters were so successful at killing these big-game animals that their population increased quickly. Researchers have estimated that in France the number of people grew from 15,000 to more than 50,000 during the time of this culture.

45

Tool Time!

Before the discovery of metal, *Homo sapiens* had to make tools using stone and bone. They learned that certain tools would make hunting animals and gathering food easier. Here are some of the tools that *Homo sapiens* from the Magdalenian period would have used.

CORE-AND-HAMMER SET

What every prehistoric hunter needs to ensure that he gets the best and sharpest stone flakes for his hand-ax, arrows, and spear!

- Core is obsidian stone to create strong and sharp flakes
- Antler hammer is sturdy and durable, with a long handle that fits comfortably in the hand
- Stone flakes are multipurpose objects that can be used as hand-axes or arrow tips
- Essential part of every hunter's toolkit
- Set comes with a handy leather travel pouch

Antler hammer

Flint flake

Prepared rock core

BURIN

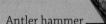

BONE HARPOON

The harpoon greatly improves the chance of hunting success. This new model is a streamlined and effective gadget that will never fail.

- Angle of teeth has been carefully calculated to ensure maximum resistance—once the harpoon has met its target, it cannot be removed easily
- Lightweight harpoon can easily be attached to spears for accurate aim when targeting an animal from a distance
- Can be used multiple times and is a must-have for every hunter

SCRAPER

Don't be caught short without the new Stone Scraper 5000! This innovative device will make animal-skinning quick and easy so that you can have your dinner cooking or your fur blanket ready in no time!

- Flat side glides effortlessly between the hide and meat of your chosen animal, with only minimal pressure required
- Perfect for cleaning animal hides
- Razor-sharp edge will leave the skin smooth and ready to use

The perfect precision tool for the prehistoric artist, this utensil is essential for creating intricate carvings on wood, or bone weapons and instruments.

- Razor-sharp point is excellent for carving delicate pictures but is also strong enough to chip away large chunks of wood or bone
- New lightweight model is slim and comfortable to hold

Facial Reconstruction

When scientists find an ancient skull, they can do a facial reconstruction that enables them to see what the owner of the skull looked like. Here is how they do it.

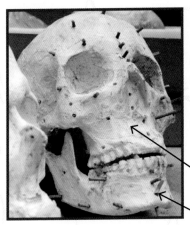

1 Pegs are inserted over a cast of the skull. These show the depth of facial flesh on a person of the same sex and age.

cast of well-preserved skull

pegs inserted by modeler

2 Clay is built around the temples and jaw, representing the muscles and underlying flesh.

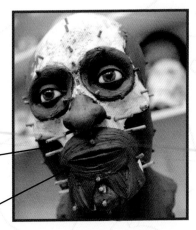

clay built up on skull

face starts to take shape

3 When the pegs are completely covered, the clay (representing the skin) is smoothed over the whole skull.

clay added to full depth

shape of nose is guessed at

facial features guessed at

4 The biggest guesses must be made in the final stages, when the hair and other features are added.

Are You a Hunter or a Gatherer?

Many behaviors people display today date back to our hunter-gatherer ancestors. Which behaviors have you inherited? Take this quiz to see whether you are a hunter or a gatherer.

1 You are on a road trip but are lost and do not know which way to go. What do you do?

a. Use a map to figure out how to get there.

b. Stop and ask for directions.

c. Go wherever the road takes you.

2 You go to the shopping mall to buy a new pair of shoes. What is your strategy?

a. You always buy the same shoes from the same store—you head straight there and get it over with.

b. You look in several different stores and try on six pairs before making a decision.

c. You do not buy shoes; you make them!

3 Your little brother borrows something without asking. How do you react?

a. You become angry and confront him.

b. You tell him politely to ask you first next time.

c. You are not interested in material possessions. He can keep it!

4 Your dad has misplaced his glasses. Are you able to help him?

a. Nope. You know he was wearing them a second ago, but you do not have a clue where they are either.

b. Of course! You have a perfect memory of him leaving them on the table in the living room.

c. Maybe. You suggest he try reading through two glasses from the kitchen.

5 A friend calls you up to arrange to go to the movies. How does it go?

a. You agree on a time and hang up. You have nothing else to say!

b. You launch into a conversation and end up on the phone for an hour.

c. You don't use phones; you communicate telepathically!

6 Which of these sports would you rather play?

a. Soccer

b. Horseback riding

c. Hide-and-seek

ANSWERS:

MOSTLY As: You are a hunter. You excel at remembering points in the landscape, confronting wild animals, competition, and solving problems.

MOSTLY Bs: You are a gatherer. Your strengths are searching for the best fruit bushes, taking care of people, remembering where things are, and getting along with others.

MOSTLY Cs: You are something else! You do your own thing and will not be pigeonholed.

Book Review
by Maggie Ian, Books Editor

Title: *Stig of the Dump*

Author: Clive King

Publisher: Puffin

Clive King's *Stig of the Dump* is an enduring modern classic. King tells the imaginative and captivating story of a boy and his secret best friend—a caveman called Stig.

First published in 1963, *Stig of the Dump* introduces a boy named Barney, who tumbles down to the bottom of an old, disused chalk quarry and finds Stig living at the bottom. Stig comes up with a wealth of innovative ways for recycling all of the junk that people throw into the quarry into building his den.

He even adds some useful and surprisingly modern features, such as a chimney and some plumbing.

The friends embark on a range of exciting adventures, each more entertaining and enthralling than the last. King is wonderful at drawing the reader into the story and at making Stig and Barney's escapades come alive, all the while infusing their tale with both humor and warmth.

Together, you, Stig, and Barney will come face-to-face with a leopard who has escaped from the zoo, catch some burglars breaking into Barney's grandparents' house, and join a fox hunt (while protecting the fox). You will even travel back to prehistoric times with Stig to help his people erect one final standing stone before the sun comes up.

Delightful exploits aside, *Stig of the Dump* is, most importantly, a story about friendship and the carefree experience of childhood. Stig may be from the Stone Age, but his loyalty and spirit are timeless.

Imaginative yet believable, funny, adventurous, and heart warming, it's a fantastic story for the young— and the young at heart.

CLIVE KING

STIG
of the Dump

PUFFIN MODERN CLASSICS
Everyone's favourite stories

Stig is described as someone with a lot of shaggy hair and two bright black eyes. He wears a rabbit skin and speaks in grunts.

CHAPTER FOUR
Gatherers

Early Magdalenians in southwest France found shelter in caves and rock ledges high above the valley floor. South-facing caves were preferred because this offered warmth from the sun's rays. Later, the people chose low-lying caves and rock shelters close to shallower crossings in the river. These were ideal positions for going out to fish and to ambush animals crossing the river. Animal hides, probably hung from stone loops hammered into the walls, would have provided a doorway to keep out the cold drafts.

Campsites have also been found near rivers, the shores of large lakes, and springs. These would have been used as hunting camps for a short while, when the group were following a migrating herd or collecting materials. The huts were made by placing large stones in a circle around a large central hearth for a fire. A light wooden frame may have been constructed and then covered with animals' skins. These were held down by the large stones. Rock slabs laid side by side formed hut floors and provided a dry surface above the ground. Archeologists think there were specific areas inside the hut used for certain activities, such as repairing tools, making flints, and sleeping. The huts varied in size with most being around 9 feet across, but the remains of some that have been found would have been double that size.

The Magdalenians were hunter-gatherers, who made the most of what their environment offered them. Everything they ate and used was taken from the wild.

Forests were young in the times of the Magdalenian, but becoming thicker. Most of the trees were pine or birch, and these provided shelter from the cold for birds and small mammals. Creatures such as mice and hares scurried around the undergrowth, while owls would swoop down to scoop up their prey.

The growing forests provided a rich resource of supplies and food for the Magdalenians as well. Wood was needed to build their camps and keep their fires burning. Branches from trees and shrubs were shaped and sharpened into useful tools and weapon handles. They attached feathers from birds to their spears for

even better flight. Bird eggs made
a tasty change from meat. Rocks and
stones were used to make structures
and tools. Bones, antlers, and animal
skins were crafted into tools, clothing,
ornaments, and home furnishings.
Plants such as grasses could have
also been used for making mats and
baskets. Just like the people living in
the Arctic today, the Magdalenians
were resourceful.

Researchers find it tricky to know how much plants were part of the early people's diet, because very little remain of these. However it is very likely that the people made the most of what they could find to eat in the forests in addition to their main diet of meat.

Like the wild boars, voles, and grouselike birds, the gatherers would find a variety of food on the forest floor at different times of the year. Many of the plants gardeners consider today to be annoying weeds were a great source of nourishment. In the spring and summer, the raw, sweet plant bulbs and fleshy young leaves were ideal for chewing. In the fall, juicy berries from rowan and blackthorn bushes were abundant. These fruits were eaten fresh or dried for storing in preparation for the winter months. Nuts such as stone pine nuts were a great source of carbohydrates, fats, and fibers, and the gathered seeds were rich in protein.

From passing down knowledge and experience, the gatherers knew which wild mushrooms to collect and which to avoid so as not to become ill. In winter, they chewed and cooked roots and tubers, which contained the much-needed energy to keep going despite the cold. These were dug up with digging sticks and then knifelike tools were used to peel and slice them.

One of the greatest challenges for the Magdalenians was to survive the harsh winter months. To keep warm, the thick coats from reindeer and other animals were used to make bedding and clothes. Tools were designed to polish the stretched hides and sew the pieces together. Stone awls had sharp points to pierce holes in the hides in preparation for sewing pieces together. Eyed needles made from bone were used to thread animal sinews, bark fibers, or cord through the holes. In this way they would have made not only warm clothes with thick hoods but also shoes and cozy boots.

60

They also liked wearing accessories such as beaded necklaces and bracelets, and even sewed shells directly onto their clothing. Many of the ivory, fossils, teeth, and bones used for decoration came from local animals. The shells may have been traded with other people who lived by the coast as they passed through.

Not only did people wrap themselves in warm clothes, they also knew how to keep warm by making fires. They gathered some short, dry twigs, and built them into the shape of a small cone, with an open face directed into the wind. Some dry moss and sticks were placed inside it. By scraping a blade flake and striking a flint skillfully, a spark from the strike caught the moss on fire. The wind fanned the flames, and within a few moments, they had a warming and glowing fire, which was also used to cook over.

The Magdalenians adapted very well to the cold, dry climate. A large crackling fire burned brightly, welcoming the hunters arriving back at the rock shelter or at camp. The smell of crushed herbs, gathered by the women, lingering in the air. Even the eerie "chow" cry of yellow-billed alpine choughs, crowlike birds, in the barren snow-covered forests in winter would not have lowered their spirits.

What were stone awls used for?

63

HUNTER-GATHERER
Four Seasons Restaurant

At the Hunter-Gatherer Restaurant, we pride ourselves on offering the finest seasonal fare. We aim to give customers an authentic "back-to-nature" experience.

SPRING
❄

Appetizer
Sautéed mice

Main course
Minted horse steak with root vegetable purée

Dessert
Fresh strawberries (v)

SUMMER
❄

Appetizer
Dried fish slices

Main course
Salmon parcels with a peppery watercress salad

Dessert
Squashed blackberries (v)

All produce is organic and responsibly sourced from the land around the Dordogne River.

FALL

❄

Appetizer
Root vegetable soup (v)

Main course
Bison and truffle hotpot

Dessert
Apple and walnut
salad (v)

WINTER

❄

Appetizer
Duck satay skewers

Main course
Spit-roasted reindeer

Dessert
Walnuts with berries (v)

WEEKDAY SPECIALS
Beetle-larva canapés
Mammoth stew
Nuts with honey

BEVERAGES

❄

Mineral water
Crushed berries
Ox blood

RESERVATIONS
To make a reservation,
please e-mail us at
reservations@hunter.gatherer.com

(v) suitable for vegetarians

Build a Cozy Bivouac

The Magdalenians used the natural resources around them to make their shelters. If you ever find yourself out in the woods, needing shelter, here is how to make a **bivouac** of your own.

1. Wedge a forked branch in the ground and place a long, sturdy pole in the fork, with the other end in the ground. Check that it is long enough to sleep under, with about 2 ft (60 cm) to spare.

2. Create an A-frame for the door by resting sturdy poles diagonally opposite each other and meeting at the fork. If necessary, use twine or plant stems to tie the main frame together.

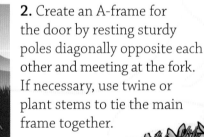

3. Lean short poles against the ridge, checking that you have room to lie down inside and to turn over in your sleep. Be sure that they do not protrude more than 1½ in. (4 cm) above the ridge pole.

4. If you have a sheet, drape it over the top and hold it down with rocks or sharp sticks. If not, cover the poles with a thick layer of leaves overlapped like roof tiles so that they do not let any rain through.

5. Hold the leaves down with a covering of thin brushwood. Pile dry grass or pine needles inside the shelter to prevent you from losing heat through the ground. Then slide in and block the entrance.

Light a Campfire

Another thing you will need in the woods is a fire. This will help scare off animals that might harm you, provide light, keep you warm, and cook food. Here is how to make one.

YOU WILL NEED THESE ITEMS:

firewood

flint*

piece of iron pyrite (fool's gold)*

tinder (dead leaves or grass)

*You can use matches, if you do not have pyrite and flint.

1 Create a platform of sticks. Lay two thick logs parallel to each other on the edges of the platform.

2 Start building layers of sticks between the logs. Each layer should be at a right angle to the last. As the construction grows, you can place tinder in the central space.

3 You will need four, five, or even six layers built on top of one another, depending on the thickness of the wood.

4 Use the flint to strike the piece of iron pyrite near the tinder. This should produce sparks to light the tinder.

You now have a fire!

Warning! Get an adult to help you.

Survival Kit

Compass
To figure out which
direction you are going in.

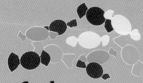

Flashlight
To find your way
in the dark.

Whistle
To call for help, so
rescuers can find you, or
to frighten animals away.

Candy
In an emergency,
these provide
a quick boost
of energy.

Fishing line and hooks
For catching your own
food: you can't bring it
all with you!

When the Magdalenians set off for the forest, they took a kit containing various tools made of flint and bone. If you go into the woods, you will need a kit of your own with many different things; here are a few of them.

Magnifying glass

For taking a closer look at the map. It can also be used to magnify the light of the sun in order to light a fire.

Small pan

For cooking food you have brought and food you catch.

Duct tape

For holding shelters and clothing together or to waterproof small items.

CHAPTER FIVE
Art Styles

The most exciting discoveries about the Magdalenians have been their impressive wall art and carvings. For pleasure, communication, or symbolic activity, they decorated the walls of caves, their rock shelters, boulders, stones, and tools. From the smallest crafted animal carving on a tool handle to the large masterpieces on the ceilings of a cavern, these people have amazed and baffled researchers with their artistic skill. How did they create them? What creative effects did they use?

Some of the earliest images were of human hands. Just like a young child fascinated by making marks, those people before the Magdalenians would spray paint using a blow pipe around their hands. They may have copied the scratch marks left on walls by cave bears and lions, experimenting with scratching the rock themselves to create the designs. However, the Lascaux cave shows a remarkable development in creating animal images that look almost alive.

Some large artworks were drawn high above the cave floor. To reach these areas, holes at the same level cut into the rock on both sides of a passage have been found. These were packed with wet, sticky clay and wooden poles pushed in to build scaffolding. A wooden platform was tied together to make secure.

Stones have been found with scratch marks on them. Just like an artist would do today, these may have been the rough sketches before the Magdalenian artists' went on to draw on the wall. The artists outlined an animal first, scratching with bones or stones, or with charcoal (burned sticks) from a fire. Then they filled in the drawings with color.

These colors, or pigments, were made from grinding different minerals (colored dirt) to powder. They only had a few minerals available to use: red iron-rich rock (**ocher**), white chalk, and black manganese ore. From these minerals, they were able to create shades of color, ranging from yellow to brown and black. These **pigments** were then mixed with liquids of cave water, animal fat, vegetable juices, or egg white to form a paste. The colored paste was then transferred to a long flat bone to act like an artist's palette.

Many outlines were made by scratching away the rock surface with a sharp stone to make engraved lines. Stencils to outline a shape were also thought to have been used. For drawing and painting, the outline color was applied using fingers or frayed sticks that had been softened by chewing to make a brush. Other brushes were perhaps made from moss, feathers, and hair. One of the ways these outlines were then filled

in was by blowing powders through tubes carved out of bird bones.
The spray of paint gave the art texture.

Some researchers have suggested that some art found was done by children or apprentices learning how to develop the skills for creating the large pieces of art. For some of the larger pieces, the artists would certainly have needed assistants to mix the paint, make the brushes, and keep the torches glowing.

Fire-lit branches, used as torches, would be swiped on the walls to relight. Sandstone lamps fueled with animal fats and lichen as wicks also provided light in the darker areas of the caves. In the flickering lamplight, the animals look as if they're moving. Most are large plant-eating animals such as aurochs, horses, deer, and bison, but some carnivores (meat-eaters) such as lions are drawn as well.

Just like professional artists today, the Magdalenian artists show that they have used both their observations studying these actual animals as well as their memory of other images they have seen to create and inspire their artworks. The animals are drawn from the side and the artists have added details of hair, face features, and used realistic coloring. The curve and roughness of the walls has been used to create a 3-dimensional effect.

Many of these animals are drawn larger than life. Some of the bulls at Lascaux are over 20 feet long. Surprisingly, although the animals look so natural, the few drawings of humans were shown as stick figures.

Researchers have been particularly baffled by the many hundreds of **geometric** designs and patterned markings. Some symbols are grouped together but others appear on their own or in pairs. There are all sorts of shapes used: triangles, squares, circles, lines, crosses, and groups of dots. Some are simple like a row of parallel lines like fingers, while others are more complex, such as groups of circles that look as if they represent huts.

Were these symbols some sort of code? They have been interpreted as possibly communicating where traps were for hunting, or representing animal tracks to show where the migrating herds were going. Some have looked like growing plants, and others like spears, harpoons, and other hunting tools. Or some of them may just be the markings of children, dabbing their fingers and brushes in paint and running them over the walls to make these decorative patterns.

The Magdalenians also showed impressive skills in carving. Tools were decorated with great care. The shoulder bones of horses or deer were ideal to use. With the sharp edge of a burin, the shapes of animals were carved into the bone. Reindeer were often shown on these objects (even though they were not often drawn on cave walls). The animals were often shown as if running with their front legs pointing back with tails upward. The heads were not in scale with the body and the animals' eyes were made larger. The carver may have been trying to give the animals character.

Other carvings found have included sandstone lamps decorated with geometric patterns, and small sculptures of animal and human figures made from stone, bone, and ivory. The small animal figures may have been placed on top of staffs (wooden sticks to help with walking and climbing). The animals' manes were shown with cross-hatching lines, but otherwise few details were added to the figures.

Carvings were perhaps the owners' way of personalizing their own tools and belongings.

What tool was used for carving pictures on bone?

Unexplained Symbols

Scientists have found repeating symbols in cave art around the world. The percentages of sites that contain each symbol are given below. It is not known what these symbols mean.

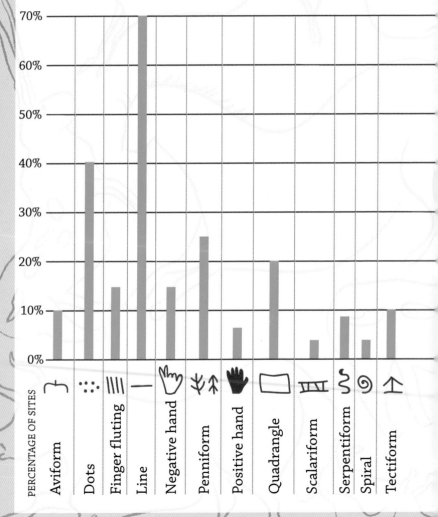

Painting in the Axial Gallery at
Lascaux showing typical symbols.

Quadrangle and lines

Aviform

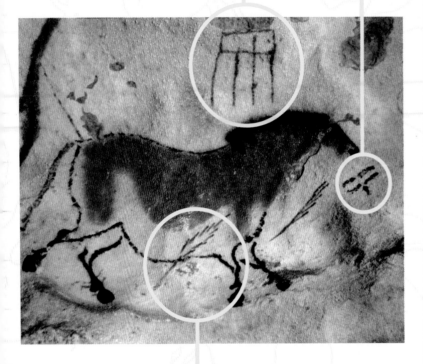

Penniform

Rock Art from Around the World

Rock art was not just in France—it was all over the world! Here is some rock art from cultures across the globe.

**Oenpelli, Arnhem Land, Australia
Date uncertain**

Plant and mineral pigments were used in ancient Aboriginal rock art, such as this painting of a turtle.

**Inanke Cave, Zimbabwe
10,000–3,000BCE**

This painting by the San people of southern Africa depicts antelope, which are believed to provide a link with the spirit world.

Fossum, Sweden
1,700–500BCE

These rock carvings show men, deer, and boats. The boats may symbolize the sea or the sun's daily journey.

Bhimbetka, India
c.10,000BCE–c.500CE

This painting on the inner wall was made using vegetable pigments and shows a procession of warriors on horses.

Make Cave Art: Creating Colors

You can make your own cave art just like the paintings at Lascaux. Here is how to do it.

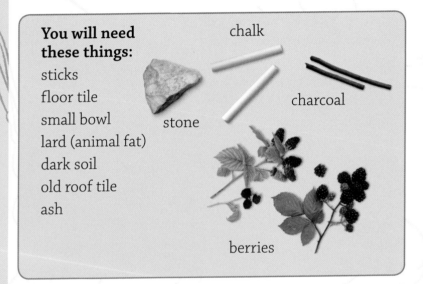

You will need these things:

sticks
floor tile
small bowl
lard (animal fat)
dark soil
old roof tile
ash

chalk

stone

charcoal

berries

1 Crush the berries. Using a stick, mix them with a little water to make a smooth red paste.

stick

berries

2 Mix the dark soil with a spoonful of lard. Add more soil to make the "paint" darker and less greasy, or more lard if the paint is too dry.

lard

dark soil

stone

3 Using the roof tile as a slab, crush the chalk with a stone, grinding it to a powder. Mix this powder with water to make a white paste.

chalk

roof tile

4 Mix the ash with a little water to make a gray paste, adding more water or ash to get the right texture.

ash

Make Cave Art: Get Painting!

5 With charcoal or a burned stick, draw a bison's body on your floor tile. Use simple lines and straight-sided shapes.

charcoal

6 Draw a triangle with stick horns for the head, and add a stick man in front of the animal, running away.

berry and soil paste

7 With your fingers, fill in the bison with the brown paint made by mixing the berry and soil pastes together. Use plenty of paste. It darkens as it dries.

8 Mix the chalk and ash pastes. Smudge this onto parts of the face and back to highlight these areas.

chalk and ash paste

9 Use a charcoal stick to darken the hooves and the end of the tail.

Your finished piece

CHAPTER SIX
Rituals

Some caves such as Lascaux are thought to have served a special purpose. Were these the places where many groups came together for rituals, special occasions, and social events such as marriages? Archeologists have searched for meanings and connections from the markings on the cave walls. Images were drawn over other images. Does this just mean they were drawn thousands of years apart or was there some meaning about where the paintings have been positioned and what has been drawn? A few of the paintings at Lascaux were near the entrance, but most were in the darker passageways and deeper chambers. They were not easily seen so these artworks were not intended as decoration for people to enjoy. Instead, like the tomb art of the later ancient Egyptians, this art may have had a more spiritual and magical reason for being drawn.

From the entrance of the Lascaux cave, a great chamber opens up perhaps as a gathering area. At certain times of the year, some natural sunlight would reach this area. This gallery, called the Hall of the Bulls, is covered in lines of aurochs and horses, but also features stags, a bear, and a strange unicorn. The unicorn (shown on page 93) appears pregnant and also has two horns, some black circles, and a red smudge over three lines. Was this a mythical guardian of the animals?

Throughout the cave network, some chambers and passageways have more artwork than others. This may mean that certain areas were more important or more sacred. Or it may just be because some places had softer walls and ceilings so engraving was easier to do on them. There are nearly 400 paintings, engravings, and symbols in the decorated passageway leading off from the hall. The layering of images may show that the same rituals were happening year after year.

Researchers have given names to the big paintings. In the Axial Gallery, or Painted Gallery, there is the huge 17-foot-long Great Black Bull, and among the other animals, the three Chinese Horses, the Falling Cow, the Fleeing Horse, and the Upside-down Horse at the end. The Black Stag represents the extinct giant deer, Megaloceros, with its majestic antlers.

In the sloping passageway called the Nave, there is the Panel of Seven Ibexes, the Panel of the Great Black Cow, the Crossed Bison, and the Frieze of the Swimming Stags. However, for the Magdalenians, the experience of viewing these masterpieces was not like visiting an art gallery with labels to explain the titled paintings. These images had some deeper significance.

Did these animals symbolize the spirit of living animals? By painting the animals were the people hoping for successful hunting in the months ahead? Some animals are shown with symbolic arrows on them, but not all. Also, many of the animals almost look as if they are prancing rather than fleeing from hunters. Many of these majestic animals are painted high on the walls, looking down over the people.

Another suggestion for where some of the paintings have been placed is due to the sound effects created in those areas. The shape of the low passageways and the height of the chambers affect the sound of humming and chanting. Experiments have shown that in certain rooms painted with clusters of animals, the sounds become louder and clearer. In other areas with less art, the sounds can hardly be heard. This creates interesting and dramatic effects.

Simple instruments such as ivory flutes and bull-roarers have also been found in caves. The holes on the flutes were precisely positioned to play notes. Roarers were long, flat instruments that whirred as they were spun around. Music to the Magdalenians was a part of sacred rituals and social gatherings, as it is for people who worship and go to parties and concerts today.

Researchers have also noticed that on some of the paintings of the bulls, dotted patterns have matched star patterns. In the Hall of the Bulls, a line of four dots were like those on the star constellation of Orion, and a cluster of dots around the eye of another bull were like the star cluster in the constellation Taurus, the Great Bull. Were these maps of the night sky?

Prehistoric rituals were part of the yearly cycle of these early people. Many of the footprints found in the Lascaux cave belonged to young people around 12 years old. This was likely to be the age of initiation from childhood to adulthood.

Handprints on cave walls have further baffled researchers. Were these the hands of the artists, leaving a signature, or do they mean something else? Many women's hands have been identified as well as men's. There have been more left hands found than right, and some even show missing fingers or signs of injury, but maybe these fingers were purposely bent. Could they be a form of sign language to communicate a message?

Other rituals may have included the burying of their dead in graves. Some of the corpses found were covered with red ocher and laid curled up and lying on their left side, or on their back. Shells and engraved deer teeth were sewn onto some of their clothing as decoration perhaps so that they could be worn for eternity. Possibly the more important the person, the more ornaments were attached.

What were some corpses covered with before they were buried?

The most ceremonial artifacts in Lascaux cave are found in a semi-circular chamber called the Apse. This is thought to have been the most sacred room. At one end, hundreds of images are particularly crowded together, leading to a 16-foot drop called the Shaft. In this deepest, most confined space is an unsual drawing.

Unlike the other artwork in the cave, or in other caves, this painting shows a story scene and features a human. Next to an outline of a roughly drawn bison, with its bowels spilling out, lies a human figure with a bird's head. A spear and a staff with a bird on the top are drawn nearby. Was this person killed by a bison on a hunting expedition? Did the people think that dead people became birds? Or does the picture show a bird-headed man performing a ritual where a bison has been killed as a sacrifice? This story scene is one of the most studied and debated pieces of artwork in the Lascaux cave.

On the other side of the figure stands a more realistic-looking woolly rhinoceros and a pattern of six black dots. No one knows if this was meant to be part of the bison scene, but more likely it was drawn at a later time. The only other image in the Shaft is a black horse. The actual, imaginary, or symbolic event conveyed by the artwork has been lost forever.

Prehistoric rituals were probably led by a **shaman** or sorcerer. This was a person who the people believed communicated with the spirit of the animals. Dressed in the headdress and cloak of an animal, the shaman would enter a trancelike state. This may have been caused by the stifling atmosphere inside the cave. The shaman would call forth the spirit of an animal for healing and guidance for the people.

The bird-headed figure in the Shaft may have been a **depiction** of a shaman. In the Apse, faintly engraved beneath a painting of a large black cow is another image of a tepeelike hut with a figure with a bird's head peeping out. Was this another shaman?

The most famous figure painting from the time of the Magdalenian is called the Sorcerer at the Trois Frères cave. In one of the deepest chambers, called the Sanctuary, the part-human, part-animal horned figure looks down on a herd of animals below. Was this a cult-god or a dancing shaman wearing a mask and antlers of a deer? The magical rituals of the Magdalenian people can only ever be debated.

THE BEST OF

THE
HOMO SAPIENS

Paleolithic Entertainment presents

I ♥ HS

The Homo Sapiens are world renowned for their spiritual performances, which have been described by many as "out of this world." The voice was the first musical instrument used by the Homo Sapiens. Their unique sound makes use of feet-stamping, clapping, and haunting ritual chanting. All instruments played in the band are handmade with natural materials, sourced from bones and tree trunks.

THE MUSICIANS

Max Homo Sapien, lead singer. He began singing as soon as he learned to talk. He is skilled at humming and imitating animal sounds.

Leo Homo Sapien on bone whistle. Leo's whistle was made by boring holes into hollow animal bone.

Sue Homo Sapien, hand-clapper. Clapping is used to create rhythm in songs and chants.

Dan Homo Sapien on the horn. Dan blows through his animal horn to make a trumpet sound.

Jen Homo Sapien on the drums. Animal skin has been stretched over hollow tree trunks or wooden frames so that Jen can hit it with hands or sticks to help keep rhythm.

THE HOMO BEST OF SAPIENS

Catching Up with Shaman Ray

Hi, I'm Peter Stein, and welcome to *Catching Up*, the show that brings you up close with Lascaux's most illustrious citizens. Today I'm meeting Shaman Ray and hearing about his out-of-this-world experiences. Welcome, Shaman Ray. So, what exactly does a shaman do?

Thank you, Peter. I organize and manage ceremonies and lead rituals for the clans. I can also cure illnesses and provide counseling using my special powers. I am greatly respected and powerful and receive gifts from the people in return.

How did you become a shaman?

I received my special powers in an inspirational moment. Some shamans are born with their powers, while others gain them through training. We are all specially chosen by the spirits, though.

What special powers do you have?

Through a state of **trance**, I enter the animal spirit world, and the spirits transfer their powers to me. With these powers, I can tell the future, diagnose and cure illnesses, and cast magical spells for successful hunting. Other skills include singing, dancing, magic tricks, and ventriloquism (throwing my voice).

Which animal spirits have helped you?

My spirit is the stag, but this is sometimes combined with the bison's spirit. Other shamans become fish, bird, unicorn, or rhinoceros spirits. There are also some who transform into a combination of ibex and horse, or bison and boar spirits.

What's it like to be in a trance?

I can't remember. The spirit takes over, and I am not myself, so I have no recollection of the event after it.

Star Map

The marks on the bull's eyes on page 79 may represent the star constellation Taurus and the Pleiades star cluster. These can be seen in the sky in the winter in the Northern Hemisphere. Take a look at this star map for February and see if you can find Taurus and the Pleiades in the sky at night, just as the people of Lascaux may have done.

URSA MAJOR

LEO

Regulus

Ecliptic

HYDRA

VIRGO

VEL

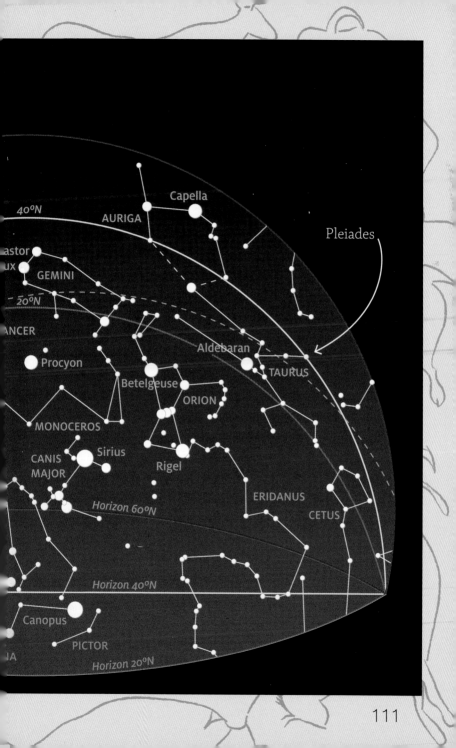

Pleiades

40°N

AURIGA

Capella

astor
ux

GEMINI

20°N

ANCER

Procyon

Aldebaran

TAURUS

Betelgeuse

ORION

MONOCEROS

CANIS
MAJOR

Sirius

Rigel

ERIDANUS

CETUS

Horizon 60°N

Horizon 40°N

Canopus

PICTOR

Horizon 20°N

A

Crime Scene Investigation:
Liguria

A body has been found in a cave in Liguria, Italy. No one knows who it is or how it got here. The police have sent a team of forensic specialists to gather clues.

1. Skull size and shape indicate that this is the body of a *Homo sapiens*.

2. Ornaments and personal possessions suggest that the person was wealthy.

3. Teeth provide clues about the person's age. This person was about 15 years old.

4. Shape of pelvis indicates that this skeleton is male.

5. Carefully arranged body suggests ceremonial burial.

6. Length of femur (leg bone) allows for the person's height to be calculated.

7. Location of burial provides clues about nearby historical events or settlements.

8. The body was found in a bed of red ocher. The meaning of this is uncertain.

CHAPTER SEVEN
Years On

The end of the time of the Magdalenians in southwest France, around 10,000BCE, marked the end of the Stone Age. The landscape had changed dramatically from the large areas of tundra grasses and mosses to the thriving thick forests. The herds of reindeer and other big game moved north and northwest,

Fish such as salmon, pike, and trout became a larger part of the Magdalenians' diet. The barbed points and design of the bone harpoon were ideal for fishing. The people also became more reliant on small forest-dwelling mammals and birds to eat. The enclosed spaces in the forest meant that hunting techniques and tools had to be adapted. Throwing tools needed to be more accurate through the forest trees. Feathers were added to the ends of spears. The development of a bow to release these arrows was soon to come in the next culture.

With the herds gone, the people began to disperse as well. There was no need to cooperate with other groups to hunt together. There were not enough big animals to keep large groups of people fed. They spread out north and northwest across Europe to find new places to live, building more permanent huts to settle in for longer. There was more variety of animals and plants available, so the people's activities differed more from day to day. There may now have been less leisure time to paint.

There was also now no need for people to gather together for rituals and sharing hunting tactics and knowledge. Instead, trading wares with people passing through became the more common way to communicate and pass on news. The Lascaux cave fell silent and the forest plants grew over the entrance.

Over 300 decorated caves and shelters have been found in France, Italy, and Spain. Archeologists still roam the landscape, searching for air currents and a distinctive smell in the rock faces that may reveal another hidden cave. The search continues to find the next discovery about the people of the Stone Age in the hope to have questions answered and theories proved.

Studies of cave art continue, trying to piece together the clues from the markings on the walls. Comparing artworks from different caves, finding similarities, and identifying the stages of development are ongoing activities. Understanding the bigger picture of the changing environment and challenges that these early people faced also helps fill in the gaps.

The story of the animals is also closely entwined with the prehistoric human story. Cave art demonstrates how much the people respected, admired, and relied on these creatures. The people recognized that their survival was dependent on the animals and inspired them. As their images of the animals gaze back at us now as we study them, our fascination with how our early ancestors lived remains alive.

How do archeologists search for hidden caves?

La Nouvelle

February 22, 1947

REVEALED: FIRST PHOTOGRAPHS OF ANCIENT FRENCH CAVE PAINTINGS

By Pierre LaRocque

Montignac, France—Ralph Morse has become the first professional photographer to capture the Lascaux cave paintings.

The caves of Lascaux were discovered several years ago, but the troubles suffered by France during World War II had kept their existence secret until a short time ago.

"I was working in the Paris bureau after the War. We received a message from New York about this cave in the south of France that people were talking about. After some investigation, we learned that the caves had been discovered during the War, but no one had ever photographed them," Morse said.

M. Parvaud, Léon Larval, Marcel Ravidat, and Jacques Marsal in Montignac, France.

The caves were first discovered on September 12, 1940, by Jacques Marsal, aged 14; Marcel Ravidat, aged 17; Georges Agniel, aged 15; and Simon Coencas, aged 13.

"It was really Robot, my dog, who discovered them," said Ravidat soon after the discovery. "We were hunting rabbits on a ridge, and Robot chased one down into a hole, so we decided to investigate."

The boys returned a few days later. Marcel was the first one in, and he described what he saw: "We came into an enormous room and raised our lanterns up. Then we saw all these big, colorful animal figures—there was a bull that was about 15 feet long. Our joy was indescribable."

The boys were the first visitors to the Great Hall of the Bulls in 17,000 years. Prehistorian Henri Breuil confirmed the authenticity of the paintings.

The boys' excitement has now been echoed seven years later, when Morse crawled into the muddy cave to take his pictures.

Of his visit, he said, "We couldn't believe what we saw. The paintings looked brand new and were absolutely enormous," Morse said.

Morse's photographs will appear in the February 24, 1947 issue of *Life* magazine.

Prehistoric Quiz

See if you can remember the answers to these questions about what you have read.

1. Approximately how long ago did the first modern humans appear?

2. What was the name of the dog who discovered Lascaux?

3. What was the name given to the people who painted at Lascaux?

4. Which early human species lived alongside *Homo sapiens*?

5. Which animal was the ancestor of today's cattle?

6. What was the main source of food for the Magdalenians?

7. What did the gatherers find to eat in the winter?

8. What were the holes in the cave walls for?

9. What were brushes made from?

10. What can the length of a skeleton's leg bone tell us about its owner?

11. In which chamber is the unicorn found?

12. What were the four animals drawn on the walls in the Shaft?

13. Who entered a trancclike state in rituals?

14. Which star cluster can be found in the constellation Taurus?

15. What hunting tool was ideal for fishing?

Answers on page 125.

Glossary

Ambush
Surprise attack made by people who are hiding.

Archeologist
Person who studies artifacts to learn about past human life.

Artifact
Object made by a human that is being studied.

Bivouac
Short-stay shelter for sleeping outside.

Depiction
Represent something in a piece of art.

Engraving
Scraping a mark on a hard surface.

Geometric
Regular lines and shapes.

Initiation
Introduction to a special group.

Migration
Seasonal movement of animals.

Ocher
Natural dirt to make colors.

Paleolithic
Period of time during the Stone Age—the earliest known age of human culture.

Pigment
Natural, dry, color powder that is mixed with water or oil to make paint.

Prehistoric
Time before writing existed.

Rituals
Actions performed during a religious ceremony.

Shaman
Person who uses magic to link the natural and supernatural worlds.

Stampede
Sudden rush of a group of frightened animals.

Trance
State of unconsciousness.

Tuber
Type of vegetable that comes from the roots of a plant.

Answers to the Prehistoric Quiz:
1. 200,000 years ago; **2.** Robot; **3.** Magdalenians; **4.** *Homo neanderthalensis*; **5.** The auroch; **6.** Reindeer; **7.** Tubers and roots; **8.** Scaffolding; **9.** Frayed sticks, moss, feathers and hair; **10.** The owner's height; **11.** The Hall of Bulls; **12.** Bison, rhinoceros, black horse, and bird; **13.** Shaman; **14.** The Pleiades; **15.** The barbed-point bone harpoon.

Index

About the Author

Deborah Lock is Senior Editor at DK, as well as a writer and mother of two. She was previously a teacher and has worked at DK since 1998, producing children's nonfiction books on all kinds of topics, from history, science, and politics to art, music, gardening, pirates, and mythical beasts. She is the series editor of the *DK Readers* reading program and is currently working on some innovative new products for the best-selling educational *Made Easy* workbooks program. She spends her leisure time involved with youth work and has a passion for singing, drama, and dancing.

About the Consultant

Dr. Linda Gambrell, Distinguished Professor of Education at Clemson University, has served as President of the National Reading Conference, the College Reading Association, and the International Reading Association. She is also reading consultant to the *DK Readers*.

Have you read these other great books from DK?

DK ADVENTURES

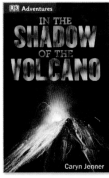

Discover the wonders of the world's deepest, darkest ocean trench.

Mount Vesuvius erupts in this adventure. Will Carlo escape?

It's a life-or-death adventure as the gang searches for a new home planet.

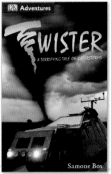

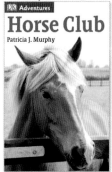

Chase twisters in Tornado Alley in this pulse-racing action adventure.

Discover what life for pilots, women, and children was like during WWII.

Emma adores horses. Will her wish come true at a riding camp?